Thanksgiv Cookbook for Cheerful Holiday

Delicious Thanksgiving Recipes That Everyone Will Love

BY: Allie Allen

COOK & ENJOY

Copyright 2019 Allie Allen

Copyright Notes

This book is written as an informational tool. While the author has taken every precaution to ensure the accuracy of the information provided therein, the reader is warned that they assume all risk when following the content. The author will not be held responsible for any damages that may occur as a result of the readers' actions.

The author does not give permission to reproduce this book in any form, including but not limited to: print, social media posts, electronic copies or photocopies, unless permission is expressly given in writing.

Table of Contents

Delicious Thanksgiving Recipes

SSSSSSSSSSSSSSSSSSSSSSSSSSSSSSSSSSSSSSSSSSSSSSSSSSSS

Chapter I - Thanksgiving Side Dishes

sssssssssssssssssssssssssssssssssssssssssssssssssssss

1) Easy Mashed Potatoes

What Thanksgiving dinner is complete without mashed potatoes? With this recipe you will make the most delicious Thanksgiving side dish that you will ever make!

Yield: 6 Servings

Cooking Time: 30 Minutes

List of Ingredients:

- 2 ½ Cups of Potatoes, Cubed and Mashed Until Smooth
- 3 Tablespoons of Milk
- 2 Tablespoons of Butter
- 1 tablespoon of Chives, Fresh and Finely Chopped
- 8 Ounces of Sour Cream
- ¼ Cup of Parmesan Cheese, Finely Grated

ssssssssssssssssssssssssssssssssssssssssssssssssssss

Procedure:

1. The first thing that you will want to do is preheat your oven to 350 degrees. While your oven is heating up use a large sized bowl and thoroughly combine your potatoes, chives, butter and milk and stir until well blended and smooth in consistency.

2. Then add in your sour cream and stir until thoroughly mixed.

3. Pour into a generously greased baking dish and top off with your grated parmesan cheese. Place into your oven to bake for at least 20 to 25 minutes or until your mashed potatoes are completely heated through. Remove from oven and enjoy immediately.

2) Garlic Flavored Green Beans

Here is yet another excellent side veggie dish that all of your guests are going to love. Even the pickiest of eaters won't be able to turn down this tasty dish!

Yield: 4 Servings

Cooking Time: 10 Minutes

List of Ingredients:

- 1 tablespoon of Butter
- 3 Tablespoons of Olive Oil
- 1 Head of Garlic, Peeled and Sliced
- 2, 14.5 Ounce Cans of Green Beans, Fully Drained
- Dash of Salt and Pepper for Taste
- ¼ Cup of Parmesan Cheese, Finely Grated

ssssssssssssssssssssssssssssssssssssssssssssssssssssssss

Procedure:

1. The first thing that you will want to do is melt your butter with your olive oil in a large sized skillet placed over medium to high heat.

2. Once your butter and oil is hot enough add in your garlic and cook until thoroughly browned.

3. Then add in your green beans and season with a dash of salt and pepper.

4. Cook your green beans for at least 10 minutes or just until the green beans become tender.

5. Once tender remove from heat and serve with a sprinkle of parmesan cheese. Enjoy!

3) Fluffy Dinner Rolls

Now this is an absolute must have for any Thanksgiving feast. These rolls are incredibly easy to make and actually do not take too much of your time to prepare.

Yield: 24 Rolls

Cooking Time: 2 ½ Hours

List of Ingredients:

- 1 Pack of Dry Yeast, Active Variety
- ¼ Cup of Water, Warm
- 1/3 Cup of Sugar, White
- ¼ Cup of Butter, Softened
- 1 teaspoon of Salt
- 1 Cup of Milk, Scalding Hot
- 1 Egg, Beaten Lightly
- 4 ½ Cups of Flour, All Purpose

sssssssssssssssssssssssssssssssssssssssssssssssssssss

Procedure:

1. First mix your yeast together with your warm water in a large sized mixing bowl. Mix until the yeast has fully dissolved.

2. Then using a separate mixing bowl combine your next four ingredients and stir constantly until your sugar fully dissolves. Allow your mixture to cool slightly before adding in your yeast mixture.

3. Next add in your egg and gradually beat in until your mixture begins to form a soft bowl. Once you have a nice dough on your hands remove from your bowl and place onto a lightly floured surface.

4. Knead your dough for the next 5 to 10 minutes to get rid of the excess gas build up and place into a generously greased bowl. Cover with some plastic wrap and place into a warm area to rise. Allow to rise for the next 90 minutes or until the dough has doubled in size.

5. After this time punch down your dough and knead again for the next 5 minutes.

6. Then shape your dough into small sized balls and place into a greased baking dish. Cover and allow to rise again until the balls have doubled in size. This should take about 35 minutes.

7. Then brush the tops of your balls with some melted butter.

8. Place your rolls into a preheated oven at 375 degrees and allow to bake for the next 18 to 20 minutes or until golden in color. Remove and allow to cool slightly before serving. Enjoy!

4) Classic Monkey Bread

Monkey Bread is a personal fan favorite in my household whenever I host Thanksgiving and I promise you it will become a fan favorite in your home as well.

Yield: 4 Servings

Cooking Time: 50 Minutes

List of Ingredients:

- 3, 12 Ounce Packs of Biscuit Dough, Cut Into Quarters
- 1 Cup of Sugar
- 2 teaspoons of Cinnamon, Ground
- ½ Cup of Margarine
- 1 Cup of Brown Sugar, Packed and Light
- ½ Cup of Walnuts, Finely Chopped
- ½ Cup of Raisins

ssssssssssssssssssssssssssssssssssssssssssssssssssss

Procedure:

1. The first thing that you will want to do is preheat your oven to 350 degrees. While your oven is heating up lightly grease a large sized Bundt pan.

2. Next toss your quartered biscuit dough into a mixture of your cinnamon and sugar, making sure that you coat the biscuits thoroughly.

3. Then place your biscuits into your pan, sprinkling with walnuts and raisins between every layer.

4. Using a small sized saucepan, melt your butter and packed brown sugar over medium heat. Bring your mixture to a boil, making sure that you stir your mixture constantly. Remove from heat and pour over your biscuits.

5. Place into your oven to bake for at least 35 minutes or until completely cooked through. Remove from oven and allow to cool before serving. Enjoy!

5) Classic Cornbread Stuffing

If you are looking to serve the most traditional Thanksgiving dinner that you can whip up, then you need to prepare a side of this stuffing. Whether it is baked in your turkey or just used as a side dish, you and your guests are going to love this recipe.

Yield: 10 to 12 Servings

Cooking Time: 30 to 45 Minutes

List of Ingredients:

- 1, 10 ½ Ounce Can of Cream of Celery Soup
- 1 Cup of Water
- ½ Cup of Butter
- 1, 10 ½ Ounce Can of Cream of Mushroom Soup
- 1 ½ teaspoons of Poultry Seasoning
- 2 Packs of Cornbread Stuffing Mix
- Some Cooking Spray

ssssssssssssssssssssssssssssssssssssssssssssssssssss

Procedure:

1. The first thing that you will want to do is preheat your oven to 350 degrees. While your oven is heating up mix both of your soups together with your water, poultry seasoning and butter in a medium sized bowl until thoroughly mixed.

2. Pour your 2 packs of cornbread stuffing into a large sized casserole dish that is generously greased with some cooking spray. Stir in your soup mixture and stir together until thoroughly moistened.

3. Cover your dish and place into your oven to bake for at least 30 minutes or until thoroughly cooked through. Remove and serve.

6) Ginger Spiced Pumpkin Bread

Here is yet another bread recipe that will go excellently with your baked turkey. It is just the kind of bread that you need to get you into the holiday spirit.

Yield: 6 Servings

Cooking Time: 1 Hour and 10 Minutes

List of Ingredients:

- 3 ½ Cups of Flour, All Purpose
- 2 teaspoons of Baking Soda
- ½ teaspoons of Baking Powder
- 1 teaspoon of Cinnamon, Ground
- 1 teaspoon of Clove, Ground
- 1 teaspoon of Allspice, Ground
- 1 ½ teaspoons of Salt
- 4 Eggs, Large in Size
- 1 Cup of Oil
- 3 Cups of Sugar, White
- 2/3 Cup of Water
- 2 teaspoons of Ginger, Ground
- ½ Cup of Pumpkin Puree

ssssssssssssssssssssssssssssssssssssssssssssssssss

Procedure:

1. The first thing that you will want to do is preheat your oven to 350 degrees. While your oven is heating up grease up a large sized baking dish with some cooking spray.

2. Then using a large sized mixing bowl add in your first 7 ingredients and mix well until evenly combined.

3. Using another medium sized bowl, combine your eggs water, sugar and oil together and beat well to evenly combine. Mix this mixture into your flour mixture to form a batter.

4. Next fold in your pumpkin and ginger and keep mixing until combined well.

5. Pour your mixture into your greased pan and place into your oven to bake for at least an hour or until fully cooked. Remove and allow to cool slightly before serving.

7) Homestyle Turkey Gravy

With this recipe you will never have to buy store bought turkey gravy ever again! This makes a wonderful addition to any Thanksgiving meal and will certainly be a side that your guests will be asking for.

Yield: 3 Cups

Cooking Time: 2 Hours

List of Ingredients:

- Some Turkey Neck and Turkey Giblet
- 2 Carrots, Medium in Size and Chopped Coarsely
- 1 Onion, Medium in Size and Cut into Quarters
- 1 teaspoon of Salt
- 1, 13 ¾ Ounce Can of Chicken Broth
- 1 tablespoon of Parsley, Fresh and Roughly Chopped
- 1 Bay Leaf
- 1 teaspoon of Thyme
- 10 Peppercorns, Whole
- 1 Cup of Heavy Cream

sssssssssssssssssssssssssssssssssssssssssssssssssss

Procedure:

1. The first thing that you will want to do is place your turkey neck, turkey giblets chicken broth and water into a medium to large sized saucepan. Heat over medium to high heat until boiling.

2. Once boiling add in your remaining ingredients except for your heavy cream and stir to thoroughly combine. Then reduce the heat to a simmer and continue to cook for at least 1 ½ hours, making sure to stir every once in a while.

3. After this time remove your turkey neck and giblets. Add in your heavy cream and whisk to evenly incorporate. Serve whenever you are ready.

8) Chipotle Style Baked Beans

While I know this is not a typical side dish that you would make alongside a tasty turkey, I promise you it is one dish that will make your entire Thanksgiving meal complete.

Yield: 4 Servings

Cooking Time: 1 Hours

List of Ingredients:

- ¼ Pound of Bacon, Finely Diced
- 1 ½ Cups of Onion, Finely Chopped
- 1/3 Cup of Brown Sugar, Dark and Packed
- 3 Tablespoons of Dijon Mustard
- 2 Tablespoons of Chipotle, Finely Chopped
- Some Chilies, Canned and In Adobo Sauce
- 5, 16 Ounce Cans of Beans, Navy Variety, Rinsed and Drained
- 1, 18 Ounce Jar of BBQ Sauce, Your Favorite Kind

SSSSSSSSSSSSSSSSSSSSSSSSSSSSSSSSSSSSSSSSSSSSSSSSSSS

Procedure:

1. The first thing that you will want to do is preheat your oven to 350 degrees.

2. While your oven is heating up, cook up your bacon in a large sized skillet over medium to high heat. Cook until your bacon is nice and crisp. Once done remove your bacon and place onto a plate lined with paper towels. Toss out most of the leftover drippings except for at least 1 to 2 tablespoons in your pan.

3. Then add in your onions into your pan and cook for at least 3 minutes. Remove from pan.

4. Then using a large sized mixing bowl combine your cooked bacon, sautéed onions and remaining ingredients and toss together until thoroughly combined. Once mixed spoon this mixture into a generously greased baking dish.

5. Place into your oven and bake for the next 45 minutes. After this time remove and serve whenever you are ready.

9) Decadent Sweet Potato Casserole

Now, I know that you are going to have some people at your dinner table that will be craving and asking for sweet potatoes and this is certainly the best dish to serve up. It is tasty and pairs excellently with a large baked turkey.

Yield: 8 Servings

Cooking Time: 1 Hour

List of Ingredients:

- 5 to 6 Sweet Potatoes, Large in Size
- 2 Eggs, Large in Size
- 1 Stick of Butter
- ½ Cup of Brown Sugar, Light and Packed
- 1 Cup of Orange Juice, Fresh
- 1 teaspoon of Nutmeg, Ground
- 1 teaspoon of Cinnamon, Ground

sssssssssssssssssssssssssssssssssssssssssssssssssssss

Procedure:

1. The first thing that you will want to do is preheat your oven to 350 degrees. While your oven is heating up take the time to boil your sweet potatoes. Once boiled drain the water and allow your sweet potatoes to cool down enough that you can handle them comfortably.

2. Once cooled peel your potatoes and mash them until they are smooth in consistency. Place into a large sized bowl.

3. Then beat in your butter (melted) and brown sugar using a mixer on the highest setting until your mixture is evenly mixed.

4. Next add in your eggs, fresh orange juice, ground nutmeg and ground cinnamon. Continue blending until smooth in consistency and evenly mixed.

5. Pour this mixture into a generously greased baking dish and place into your oven to bake for at least 25 to 30 minutes or until completely heated through. After this time remove from oven and serve at once. Enjoy!

10) Healthy Grilled Asparagus

If you are looking to add some healthy veggies to your Thanksgiving dish, then this is the best recipe to make. This asparagus is incredibly filling and incredibly tender, making it a healthy vegetable that all of your guests are certainly going to enjoy.

Yield: 4 Servings

Cooking Time: 20 Minutes

List of Ingredients:

- 2 Pounds of Asparagus Spears, Fresh
- 1 ½ Cups of Balsamic Vinaigrette Dressing
- 2 teaspoons of Lemon Zest, Finely Grated
- ¼ Cup of Parsley, Fresh and Finely Chopped
- 1 tablespoon of Butter, Melted
- ½ teaspoons of Salt
- ½ teaspoons of Black Pepper, Fresh and Ground

ssssssssssssssssssssssssssssssssssssssssssssssssss

Procedure:

1. The first thing that you will want to do is blanch your asparagus. To do this take out a large sized pot and boil a generous amount of water. Add in your asparagus and allow them to boil for at least 1 minute or until they are tender. Remove them and immediately run them under some cold water until they are cool. Place into a plastic zip lock bag.

2. Add your vinaigrette into your bag next and seal. Place into your fridge to marinate overnight.

3. The next day drain your asparagus, making sure to keep the excess dressing.

4. Place your asparagus onto a pre-heated grill and as your grill brush them with some butter, parsley, salt and pepper. Once tender remove from grill and serve alongside the leftover dressing for the tastiest results.

11) Sweet Cornbread Muffins

While many people out there are going to assume that this is a sweet tasting dessert dish, this is in fact a dish that you can serve alongside your turkey. There is nothing quite like fresh cornbread to go along with a heaping plate of turkey, stuffing and mashed potatoes!

Yield: 12 Muffins

Cooking Time: 45 Minutes

List of Ingredients:

- ½ Cup of Cornmeal, Yellow in Color
- 1 Cup of Almond Milk
- 3 Tablespoons of Vegetable Oil
- 2/3 Cups of Flour, All Purpose
- 1 to 2 Eggs, Large In Size
- 1 tablespoon of Baking Powder
- ¼ Cup of Applesauce

sssssssssssssssssssssssssssssssssssssssssssssssssssss

Procedure:

1. The first thing that you will want to do is preheat your oven to 400 degrees. While your oven is heating up grease up a few muffin pans with a generous amount of vegetable oil or cooking spray.

2. Next combine all of your ingredients together into a large sized mixing bowl and stir until thoroughly mixed.

3. Once you have your batter fill up your muffin pans with at least ¾ of your muffin batter for each cup.

4. Then place your muffin pans into your oven and bake for the next 30 minutes or until golden brown in color. Once cooked remove from oven and allow to cool slightly before serving.

Chapter II - Thanksgiving Main Dishes

ssssssssssssssssssssssssssssssssssssssssssssssssssss

12) Classic Roast Turkey

This is a class roast turkey recipe that you will want to make every year. With the help of this recipe it will be easy to make turkey for the entire family and I guarantee that they will be craving for more.

Yield: 12 Servings

Cooking Time: 4 to 5 Hours

List of Ingredients:

- 12 to 14 Pounds of Turkey, Thawed or Fresh
- Some Turkey Broth
- 2 Cloves of Garlic, Minced
- ½ Cup of Butter, Melted
- 1 tablespoon of Rosemary, Dried
- 3 Tablespoons of Flour, All Purpose
- 1 teaspoon of Salt
- ½ teaspoons of Black Pepper, Fresh and Ground

sssssssssssssssssssssssssssssssssssssssssssssssssssssss

Procedure:

1. The first thing that you will want to do is preheat your oven to 450 degrees. While your oven is preheating rinse off your turkey and pat dry with some paper towels.

2. Then prepare your stuffing however which way you like. Once you have your stuffing, make sure that you stuff the neck and body of your turkey with a generous amount of stuffing. Tie the legs of the turkey with some cotton string. Position the wings so that they rest under the turkey.

3. Next combine your minced garlic with your melted butter. Once mixed spread this mixture generously over your turkey. Place into a roasting pan.

4. Decrease the heat of your oven to 350 degrees and roast your turkey for 22 to 25 minutes per pound.

5. After an hour brush your turkey with your butter and garlic mixture and then continue to do so every 1 ½ hours.

6. Continue roasting until your turkey's internal temperature reaches at least 180 degrees. Serve once fully cooked.

13) BBQ Turkey

This is a turkey recipe that you can make when you want to change up your Thanksgiving tradition. This is a turkey recipe that I know even the pickiest of eaters are going to love and that will make your home the popular Thanksgiving household.

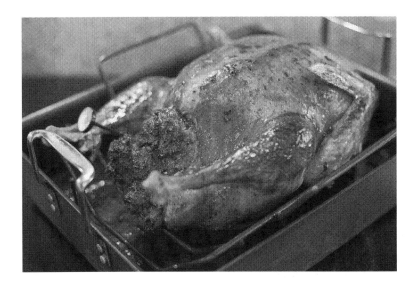

Yield: 12 Servings

Cooking Time: 5 to 6 Hours

List of Ingredients:

- 1, 13 to 14 Pound Turkey
- 7 Quarts of Water
- 2 Onions, Large in Size
- 1 Cup of Salt
- 1 Cup of Ginger, Finely Chopped
- ¾ Cup of Brown Sugar, Light and Packed
- 4 Bay Leaves, Fresh
- 12 Peppercorns, Black and Fresh
- 2 Oranges, Fresh
- ¼ Cup of Vegetable Oil
- 2 Tablespoons of Sesame Oil

Ingredients for Your Glaze:

- ¾ Cup of Honey, Pure
- ½ Cup of Wine, White
- 1/3 Cup of Dijon Mustard
- 2 Tablespoons of Butter

sssssssssssssssssssssssssssssssssssssssssssssssssss

Procedure:

1. To begin make sure that you follow this step the night before you bake your turkey. First place your first nine ingredients except for your turkey into a large sized pot. Heat this mixture under a low simmer and stir to combine until the salt and sugar fully dissolve.

2. Then take your turkey and rinse it off. Pat it dry with some paper towels. Place your turkey into a large sized roasting pan and place your cooled off sauce over it. Place your turkey into your fridge and allow it to marinate overnight.

3. The next day preheat your oven to 350 degrees. Take your orange wedges and stuff them into the body cavity of your turkey.

4. Next combine your vegetable oil and sesame oil together in a medium sized bowl. Pour this mixture over your turkey.

5. To make your glaze all that you have to do is combine all of your ingredient for your glaze together into a medium sized saucepan. Bring this mixture to a simmer and then pour all over your turkey.

6. Place your turkey into your oven to bake for at least 22 to 25 minutes per pound. Continue baking until your turkey's internal temperature reaches at least 180 degrees. Serve once fully cooked. Enjoy!

14) Easy Baked Turkey

This is the perfect turkey recipe for those who have yet to make a turkey on their own. This is a relatively easy turkey recipe to follow and it is one that all of your dinner guest will certainly enjoy.

Yield: 12 Pounds of Turkey

Cooking Time: 3 ½ to 4 Hours and 15 Minutes

List of Ingredients:

- 1, 12 Pound Turkey, Giblets Removes and Thoroughly Washed
- 6 Tablespoons of Butter, Evenly Divided
- 4 Cups of Water, Warm
- 3 Tablespoons of Chicken Bouillon
- 2 Tablespoons of Parsley, Dried
- 2 Tablespoons of Onion, Dried and Minced
- 2 Tablespoons of Salt, Seasoning Variety

sssssssssssssssssssssssssssssssssssssssssssssssssss

Procedure:

1. The first thing that you will want to do is preheat your oven to 350 degrees. While your oven is heating up place your turkey into a large sized roasting pan. Create small one inch pockets on every side of the turkey by separating the skin slightly. Place at least 3 Tablespoons of Butter into each pocket that you create.

2. Then using a medium sized bowl, combine your water and chicken bouillon together. Add in your parsley and minced onion and stir to combine. Drizzle this over your turkey. Finally season your turkey with a generous amount of your seasoning salt.

3. Cover your turkey with foil and place into your oven to bake for at least 3 ½ to 4 hours or until the internal temperature of your turkey reaches 180 degrees. During the last 45 minutes of cooking remove your aluminum foil to allow the turkey to achieve that delicious looking brown color. Once done remove from oven, carve and serve immediately. Enjoy!

15) Sweet Apricots and Ham

Ham is a great meat recipe to serve alongside your ham. Not only is ham increasingly versatile, but it compliments a side of turkey well. This certain ham recipe make a sweet tasting ham, giving it the ability to satisfy nearly any taste bud.

Yield: 3 to 4 Pounds of Ham

Cooking Time: 2 to 4 Hours

List of Ingredients:

- 1, 3 to 4 Pound Ham, Smoked and Boneless
- ½ Cup of Apricot, Preserves
- ½ Cup of Honey, Pure
- ½ Cup of Water
- 1 teaspoon of Mustard, Dry
- 1 teaspoon of Water
- 1 tablespoon of Cornstarch
- 3 Tablespoons of Lemon Juice
- ¼ teaspoons of Cloves, Ground

ssssssssssssssssssssssssssssssssssssssssssssssssssss

Procedure:

1. The first thing that you will want to do is preheat your oven to 325 degrees. While your oven is heating up, place your ham into a large sized roasting pan and add in at least 1/2 cup of water. Cover with some aluminum foil and place into your oven.

2. Roast your ham for at least 25 minutes per pound.

3. While your ham is roasting thoroughly combine your remaining ingredients until evenly mixed.

4. Then remove your ham from your oven and brush your ham with your glaze mixture. Continue to do so for at least 10 minutes before your ham is actually done cooking.

5. Remove your ham from the oven and allow to cool slightly before serving. Enjoy!

16) Succulent Cranberry Pork Tenderloin

This is a great tasting pork recipe to serve alongside your turkey that will leave all of your guests craving for more. It is coated in cranberries, making it a dinner recipe that will satisfy even the strongest of sweet teeth.

Yield: 6 Servings

Cooking Time: 50 Minutes

List of Ingredients:

- ½ Cup of Cranberries, Dried
- 1 Cup of Water
- 1 teaspoon of Vegetable Oil
- 1 Pound of Pork, Cut into Medallions
- Dash of Salt and Pepper for Taste
- 2 Tablespoons of Shallots, Minced
- ½ Cup of Wine, Tawny Port Variety
- ¼ Cup of White Vinegar, Distilled
- 1 Cup of Chicken Broth
- ½ teaspoons of Thyme, Dried
- 1 teaspoon of Cornstarch
- 1 tablespoon of Water

sssssssssssssssssssssssssssssssssssssssssssssssssssss

Procedure:

1. Using a small sized saucepan, combine your cranberries and water together. Bring over low heat and allow to simmer for at least 3 minutes. After this time drain your cranberries, making sure to save the liquid as you do so. Set the cranberries aside.

2. Then use a large sized skillet and place over medium heat. Add some oil to it. Then season your pork with a generous amount of salt and pepper and add to your skillet once the oil is hot enough. Cook your pork for about 3 minutes, then turn. Continue to cook until the pork is completely cooked through. Remove and place onto a serving plated.

3. Next add in your minced shallots to your hot skillet and allow to cook for at least 1 minute. Then add in your wine and vinegar and bring your mixture to a rolling boil, making sure to stir as frequently as possible.

4. Allow your mixture to boil for at least 4 minutes before add in your broth, drained cranberry water and dried thyme. Stir to completely combine and allow to come to a boil again.

5. Next combine your cornstarch with your 1 tablespoon of water. Then whisk into your mixture and reduce your heat to a simmer, making sure to stir occasionally until your sauce is thick in consistency.

6. Then stir in your cranberries and season with a dash of salt and pepper.

7. Remove your mixture from heat and serve on top of your cooked pork. Serve at once and enjoy.

17) Spiced Roast Turkey

Here is yet another turkey recipe that I know you are going to want to make. It is packed full of different spices, making this turkey one that is full of flavor that your entire family will love.

Yield: 12 Servings

Cooking Time: 1 Hour and 30 Minutes

List of Ingredients:

- 1, 5 Pound Turkey Breast, Boneless
- 2 teaspoons of Vegetable Oil
- 3 teaspoons of Cinnamon, Ground
- 2 teaspoons of Cloves, Ground
- 1 tablespoon of Black Pepper
- 1 Cup of Cranberries, Fresh
- 2 Cups of Water
- 3 Tablespoons of Orange Juice, Fresh
- 1 tablespoon of Cornstarch
- 2 Tablespoons of Water

ssssssssssssssssssssssssssssssssssssssssssssssssss

Procedure:

1. The first thing that you will want to do is preheat your oven to 375 degrees. While your oven is heating up rinse your turkey off and pat dry. Place into a large sized roasting pan.

2. Then grease your turkey with a generous amount of vegetable oil.

3. Next mix together your cloves, ground cinnamon and black pepper together until thoroughly combined. Spread this mix all of your turkey, making sure to season every inch.

4. Place your turkey into your oven and roast for 1 hour.

5. While your turkey is roasting, create your sauce by combining your cranberries and 2 cups of water together. Add to a medium sized saucepan and bring the mixture to a low boil. Once boiling reduce the heat to a simmer and cook just until your cranberries begin to open.

6. Then add in your orange juice, cornstarch and 2 more tablespoons of water to your sauce. Stir well until your sauce begins to thicken and remove from heat.

7. Remove your turkey from the oven and pour your sauce over the turkey slices generously.

18) Hawaiian Style Ham

This is a great tasting ham recipe that even the pickiest of eaters will enjoy. It is sweet to taste and extremely easy to make, I guarantee that you will want to make this dish for every Thanksgiving holiday.

Yield: 5 to 7 Pounds

Cooking Time: 3 to 5 Hours

List of Ingredients:

- 1, 5 to 7 Pounds of Pork Shoulder, Smoked and Fully Cooked
- 1, 15 Ounce Can of Pineapple, Finely Sliced
- ¼ Cup of Brown Sugar, Light and Packed
- ¼ Cup of Honey, Pure
- 1 Jar of Cherries, Maraschino Style
- 3 Cloves, Whole

sssssssssssssssssssssssssssssssssssssssssssssssssss

Procedure:

1. The first thing that you will want to do is preheat your oven to 350 degrees. While your oven is heating up skin your ham and then place into a large sized roasting pan.

2. Tent some aluminum foil over your ham and bake for at least 30 minutes per pound.

3. Once fully cooked remove from oven and place your pineapple slices on top. Also pour some of your pineapple juice over the top of the ham. Allow to cool for at least 20 minutes before servings. Enjoy!

19) Cranberry Stuffed Turkey Breast

If you are looking to make a different type of turkey dish this Thanksgiving, then this is the perfect turkey recipe for you. This is a tasty twist to a traditional Thanksgiving dish that I am for certain you are going to want to make every year.

Yield: 4 Servings

Cooking Time: 1 Hour and 30 Minutes

List of Ingredients:

- 1, 12 Ounce Pack of Stuffing Mix, Herb Seasoned Bread Variety
- 2 Turkey Breasts, Skinless and Boneless
- 1 Cup of Pecans, Finely Chopped
- 2, 8 Ounce Packs of Cranberries, Dried
- 1 tablespoon of Butter, Fully Melted
- 6 Leaves of Lettuce
- ½ Cup of Pecan Halves

sssssssssssssssssssssssssssssssssssssssssssssssssss

Procedure:

1. The first thing that you have to do is preheat your oven to 425 degrees.

2. While your oven is heating up cut your turkey breasts butterfly style and then lay flat onto a pan lined with wax paper. Cover your turkey with another piece of wax paper and pound your turkey breasts as flat as possible.

3. Next spread your stuffing along the edge of each turkey breast and sprinkle with your dried cranberries and chopped pecans. Then roll up your turkey breasts similar to a jellyroll. Tuck the ends of the breasts on the inside and tie off with some kitchen string.

4. Place your completed turkey breasts onto a baking dish that is generously greased and baste your turkey with some butter.

5. Place your turkey into your oven and bake for the next 15 minutes. After this time reduce the heat to 350 degrees and continue to bake for another 35 to 45 minutes or until your turkey reaches an internal temperature of 170 degrees.

6. Once cooked remove your turkey and slice into thick rounds. Serve right away and enjoy!

Chapter III - Thanksgiving Desserts

ssssssssssssssssssssssssssssssssssssssssssssssssssssss

20) Chocolate Cheesecake

This is one cheesecake recipe that every chocolate lover will fall in love with. It is incredibly decadent and absolutely delicious, this is one dessert recipe that you will want to make over and over again.

Yield: 1 Cake

Cooking Time: 2 Hours

Ingredients for Your Crust:

- 1 ½ Cups of Cookie Crumbs, Chocolate
- 1/3 Cup of Powdered Sugar
- 1/3 Cup of Cocoa Powder
- ¼ Cup of Butter

Ingredients for Your Filling:

- 3, 8 Ounce Packs of Cream Cheese, Softened
- 1 ¼ Cups of Sugar, White
- ¼ Cup of Cocoa Powder
- 3 Tablespoons of Flour, All Purpose
- 3 Eggs, Large in Size
- ½ Cup of Sour Cream
- ¼ Cup of Bailey's

sssssssssssssssssssssssssssssssssssssssssssssss

Procedure:

1. The first thing that you will want to do is preheat your oven to 350 degrees.

2. While your oven is heating up use a medium sized bowl to combine your first 4 ingredients. Stir thoroughly to combine. Then press your mixture into the bottom of a generously greased spring form pan.

3. Place your pan into your oven to bake for at least 10 minutes. After this time remove from oven and set aside. Increase your oven's temperature to 450 degrees.

4. Then use a large sized mixing bowl to mix together your remaining ingredients together until smooth in consistency. Pour this mixture into your pan.

5. Bake for the next 10 minutes before reducing the heat to 250 degrees. Continue to bake your cake for at least 60 minutes. After this time remove from pan and allow to cool completely. Then place into your fridge to chill overnight.

6. Serve the next day and I highly recommend serving this cake with a few chocolate shavings for additional tastiness.

21) Spiced Sugar Cookies

This is the perfect dessert recipe to make especially if you have a bunch of little ones running around the house. These cookies are easy to make and I guarantee your little ones will be begging you for more.

Yield: 30 Cookies

Cooking Time: 2 Hours and 30 Minutes

Ingredients for Your Cookies:

- 1 Cup of Sugar, Granulated
- 2 ½ Cups of Flour, All Purpose
- 1 teaspoon of Pumpkin Pie Spice
- ¼ teaspoons of Baking Powder
- Some Fine Salt
- 12 Tablespoons of Butter, Unsalted and Cut into Small Pieces
- 1 Egg, Large in Size and Beaten Lightly
- 1 teaspoon of Vanilla Extract, Pure

Ingredients For Your Icing:

- 2 Tablespoons of Meringue Powder
- 3 ¾ to 4 Cups of Confectioners' Sugar
- Some Food Coloring, Optional

ssssssssssssssssssssssssssssssssssssssssssssssssssss

Procedure:

For Your Cookie:

1. To make your cookies first place your sugar into a few processor and pulse for a couple of minutes or until your sugar is very fine. Then add in your next four ingredients and pulse yet again to thoroughly combine.

2. Next add in your butter and continue to pulse until your mixture resembles that of sand.

3. Then add in your large and beaten egg and pure vanilla. Continue to pulse until your mixture begins to form large lumps.

4. Remove your dough from your food processor and knead on a clean surface for a few times and then shape your dough into a ball. Divide your ball of dough directly in half and flatten two large disks. Cover each disk and place into your fridge for an hour or until firm.

5. Next preheat your oven to 350 degrees. While your oven is heating up line a baking sheet with some parchment paper.

6. Next roll out your discs of dough until they are at least 1/8 inch in thickness. Then cut your dough with your favorite cookie cutters and place your newly crafted cookies onto your baking sheet.

7. Place your cookies into your oven and bake just until your cookies are golden brown in color. This should take at least 10 to 12 minutes. After this time remove from your oven and place onto a cooling rack to cool. Repeat this process as needed

For Your Icing:

1. To make your icing sift your meringue powder and sugar together in a large sized mixing bowl. Then add in at least 6 tablespoons of water.

2. Beat this mixture with an electric mixed on the highest setting or just until small peaks begin to form in your mixture. This should take at least 3 to 4 minutes. Feel free to add food coloring if you wish.

3. Decorate your cookies whichever way you want and serve your cookies when you are ready.

22) Carrot Cheesecake

This is a great desert recipe to make when you are looking to wrap up your perfect Thanksgiving dinner. It is one dessert dish that I know all of your guests are going to love.

Yield: 8 Servings

Cooking Time: 3 to 4 Hours

Ingredients for Cream Cheese Batter:

- 16 Ounces of Cream Cheese, Room Temperature
- ¾ Cup of Sugar, White
- 2 ½ teaspoons of Vanilla Extract, Pure
- 1 tablespoon of Flour
- 3 Eggs, Large in Size

Ingredients for Your Carrot Cake:

- ¾ Cup of Vegetable Oil
- 1 Cup of Sugar, White
- 2 Eggs, Large in Size
- 1 ½ teaspoons of Vanilla Extract, Pure
- 1 Cup of Flour
- 1 teaspoon of Baking Soda
- 1 ½ teaspoons of Cinnamon, Ground
- 1 teaspoon of Nutmeg, Ground
- ½ teaspoons of Ginger
- 8 Ounces of Pineapple, Crushed, Canned and Juice Reserved
- 1 Cup of Carrots, Finely Grated
- ½ Cup of Coconut, Finely Shredded
- ½ Cup of Walnuts, Finely Chopped

Ingredients for Your Pineapple Cream Cheese Frosting:

- 2 Ounces of Cream Cheese, Softened
- 1 tablespoon of Butter, Softened
- 1 ¾ Cup of Confectioner's Sugar
- 1 teaspoon of Vanilla Extract
- 1 tablespoon of Pineapple Juice, Reserved

sssssssssssssssssssssssssssssssssssssssssssssssssssss

Procedure:

For Cream Cheese Batter:

1. The first thing that you will have to do is preheat your oven to 350 degrees.

2. While your oven is heating up use a large sized mixing bowl and beat together your softened cream cheese and sugar together until smooth in consistency. Once smooth mix in your flour, eggs and pure vanilla extract until evenly mixed. Set aside.

For Your Cake Batter:

1. Use a large sized bowl and thoroughly combine your first 9 ingredients for your batter together until thoroughly combined. Then stir in your remaining ingredients until evenly mixed.

2. Pour at least 1 ½ cups of your cake batter into the bottom of a lightly greased spring form pan. Then drop spoonfuls of your cream cheese batter on top of your cake batter. Spoon your remaining cake batter over the cream cheese and top with your remaining cream cheese batter.

3. Place your pan into your oven to bake for at least 1 hour or until your cake is fully set. Once finished remove from oven and allow to fully cool by chilling for another hour.

For Your Frosting:

1. Using a medium sized bowl, cream all of your frosting ingredients together until your frosting is smooth in consistency.

2. Once your cake has fully cooled, smooth the frosting onto its surface then place back into your fridge to chill overnight.

23) Apple Spiced Cake

This is a decadent cake recipe that everybody in your household will be begging for. It is incredibly spiced and is the perfect way to end a great Thanksgiving dinner with family.

Yield: 1 Cake

Cooking Time: 2 Hours

Ingredients for Your Cake:

- ½ Stick of Butter
- 3 Apples, Granny Smith Variety, Peeled, Cored and Finely Sliced
- ½ Lemon, Fresh and Juiced
- 1 Cup of Apple Cider
- 1 ¾ Cups of Flour, All Purpose
- 1 teaspoon of Cinnamon, Ground
- 1 teaspoon of Baking Soda
- 3 to 4 Grates of Nutmeg, Fresh
- ¾ Cup of Brown Sugar, Light and Packed
- ¾ Cup of Sugar
- Dash of Salt
- 1 Egg, Large in Size
- 1 teaspoon of Vanilla Extract, Pure
- ½ Cup of Walnuts, Toasted and Finely Chopped
- ½ Cup of Raisins, Golden

Ingredients for Your Cream Cheese Icing:

- 1, 8 Ounce Pack of Cream Cheese, Room Temp.
- 1 Stick of Butter, Room Temp.
- 1 Cup of Powdered Sugar
- 1 teaspoon of Vanilla Extract

sssssssssssssssssssssssssssssssssssssssssssssss

Procedure:

For Your Cake:

1. The first thing that you will want to do is melt your butter in a large sized pan placed over medium heat. Once the butter is fully melted add in your apple and stir them to completely coat it in your butter.

2. Then add in your fresh lemon juice and apple cider. Continue to cook your apples until they are soft. Transfer this mixture into a food processor and pulse until it forms a paste.

3. Then using a large sized mixing bowl combine your next seven ingredients until thoroughly combined. Then make a well in your ingredients and add in your apple puree mixture. Add in your egg and pure vanilla extract. Stir to thoroughly combine.

4. Next toss in your finely chopped walnuts and raisins and toss again to combine.

5. Take a loaf pan and grease it with some butter and flour. Once greased add in your batter and place your pan into your oven.

6. Bake your cake for the next 40 to 45 minutes or until the cake is fully set.

7. Once set remove from oven and allow to cool completely to add your cream cheese icing.

For Cream Cheese Icing:

1. To make your icing beat all of your ingredients together until light and fluffy. Continue mixing until smooth inconsistency.

2. Spread over your cooled cake and serve your cake whenever you are ready.

24) Classic Pumpkin Pie

There is nothing more traditional for Thanksgiving then enjoying a tasty pumpkin pie. With this recipe you can make the tastiest pumpkin pie right from the comfort of your own home.

Yield: 1 Pie

Cooking Time: 2 Hour and 25 Minutes

List of Ingredients:

- 1, 15 Ounce Can of Pumpkin Filling
- 1, 14 Ounce Can of Condensed Milk, Sweetened
- 2 Eggs, Large in Eggs
- 1 teaspoon of Cinnamon, Ground
- ½ teaspoons of Ginger, Ground
- ½ teaspoons of Nutmeg, Ground
- ½ teaspoons of Salt
- 1 Pie Crust, Large in Size and Unbaked

sssssssssssssssssssssssssssssssssssssssssssssssssss

Procedure:

1. The first thing that you will want to do is preheat your oven to 425 degrees.

2. While your oven is heating up whisk together all of your ingredients except for your pie crust in a large sized bowl and blend until smooth in consistency.

3. Once smooth pour your mixture into your pie crust.

4. Place into your oven and bake for the next 15 minutes.

5. After 15 minutes reduce the temperature in your oven to 350 degrees and continue to bake your pie for at least 35 to 40 minutes. Remove from oven and allow to cool. Serve whenever you are ready.

25) Classic Apple Pie

There is nothing better than to bring in the Thanksgiving holiday with a classic and traditional Apple Pie. I promise you that this is the tastiest apple pie that you will ever taste. I guarantee that your dinner guests will fall in love with.

Yield: 1 Pie

Cooking Time: 1 ½ Hours

List of Ingredients:

- 1 Double Crust Pie Crust, Premade
- ½ Cup of Butter, Unsalted
- 3 Tablespoons of Flour, All Purpose
- ¼ Cup of Water
- ½ Cup of Sugar, White
- ½ Cup of Brown Sugar, Light and Packed
- 8 Apples, Granny Smith Variety, Peeled, Cored and Finely Sliced

ssssssssssssssssssssssssssssssssssssssssssssssssss

Procedure:

1. The first thing that you will want to do is preheat your oven to 425 degrees.

2. While your oven is heating up use a medium sized saucepan and bring it over medium heat. Add in your butter and melt it completely. Once melted stir in your flour and stir until it forms a paste.

3. Then add in your packed brown sugar, water and sugar and let your mixture come to a boil. Once boiling reduce the heat until your mixture is simmering.

4. Take your pie crusts and place them into a pie pan. Fill your crust with your finely sliced apples, making a slight mound. Cover your pie with a lattice crust.

5. Next gently pour your butter and sugar mixture over your pie crust, making sure that none of the liquid runs off of the pie.

6. Place into your oven to bake for the next 15 minutes. After this time reduce the heat to 350 degrees and continue to bake for 35 to 45 minutes or until your apples are soft. Remove from oven and allow to cool slight before serving. Enjoy!

26) Classic Rum Cake

Here is yet another great tasting dessert recipe that I know you are going to love. Incredibly decadent and sweet to taste, this is the perfect cake recipe to serve alongside some ice cream.

Yield: 1 Cake

Cooking Time: 1 Hour and 5 Minutes

List of Ingredients:

- 1 Cup of Walnuts, Finely Chopped
- 1 Package of Yellow Cake Mix
- 1 Pack of Vanilla Pudding Mix
- 4 Eggs, Large in Size
- ¾ Cup of Water, Evenly Divided
- ½ Cup of Vegetable Oil
- 1 Cup of Rum, Dark and Evenly Divided
- ½ Cup of Butter
- 1 Cup of Sugar, White

sssssssssssssssssssssssssssssssssssssssssssssssss

Procedure:

1. The first thing that you will want to do is preheat your oven to 325 degrees.

2. While your oven is heating up use a large sized bowl and stir together your cake mix and pudding mix until evenly mixed.

3. Then whisk in half of your dark rum, large eggs, oil and half of your water and blend together until evenly mixed.

4. Next pour your finely chopped walnuts into a large sized Bundt pan that is greased generously. Then pour your batter over your walnuts.

5. Place your pan into your oven and bake for the next hours or until your cake is fully set.

6. While your cake is baking use a small sized saucepan and combine your remaining water, ¼ cup of water, sugar and butter together. Bring this mixture to a boil, making sure to stir as constantly as possible. Allow your mixture to boil for at least 5 minutes before removing from heat.

7. Stir in your remaining rum into your mixture. Drizzle this over your fully baked cake and allow to cool slightly before you serve it. Enjoy!

About the Author

Allie Allen developed her passion for the culinary arts at the tender age of five when she would help her mother cook for their large family of 8. Even back then, her family knew this would be more than a hobby for the young Allie and when she graduated from high school, she applied to cooking school in London. It had always been a dream of the young chef to study with some of Europe's best and she made it happen by attending the Chef Academy of London.

After graduation, Allie decided to bring her skills back to North America and open up her own restaurant. After 10 successful years as head chef and owner, she decided to sell her business and pursue other career avenues. This monumental decision led Allie to her true calling, teaching. She also started to write e-books for her students to study at home for practice. She is now the proud author of several e-books and gives private and semi-private cooking lessons to a range of students at all levels of experience.

Stay tuned for more from this dynamic chef and teacher when she releases more informative e-books on cooking and baking in the near future. Her work is infused with stores and anecdotes you will love!

Author's Afterthoughts

I can't tell you how grateful I am that you decided to read my book. My most heartfelt thanks that you took time out of your life to choose my work and I hope you find benefit within these pages.

There are so many books available today that offer similar content so that makes it even more humbling that you decided to buying mine.

Tell me what you thought! I am eager to hear your opinion and ideas on what you read as are others who are looking for a good book to buy. Leave a review on Amazon.com so others can benefit from your wisdom!

With much thanks,

Allie Allen

Printed in Great Britain
by Amazon

68467912R00059